Viz
THE
BIG FAT SLAGS BOOK

Written and drawn by
Graham Dury and Simon Thorp.

With additional contributions by
Simon Donald and Chris Donald.

ISBN 1 870870 46 8

Published in Great Britain by John Brown Publishing Limited,
The Boathouse, Crabtree Lane, Fulham, London SW6 6LU

First Printing May 1994

Printed and bound in Great Britain.

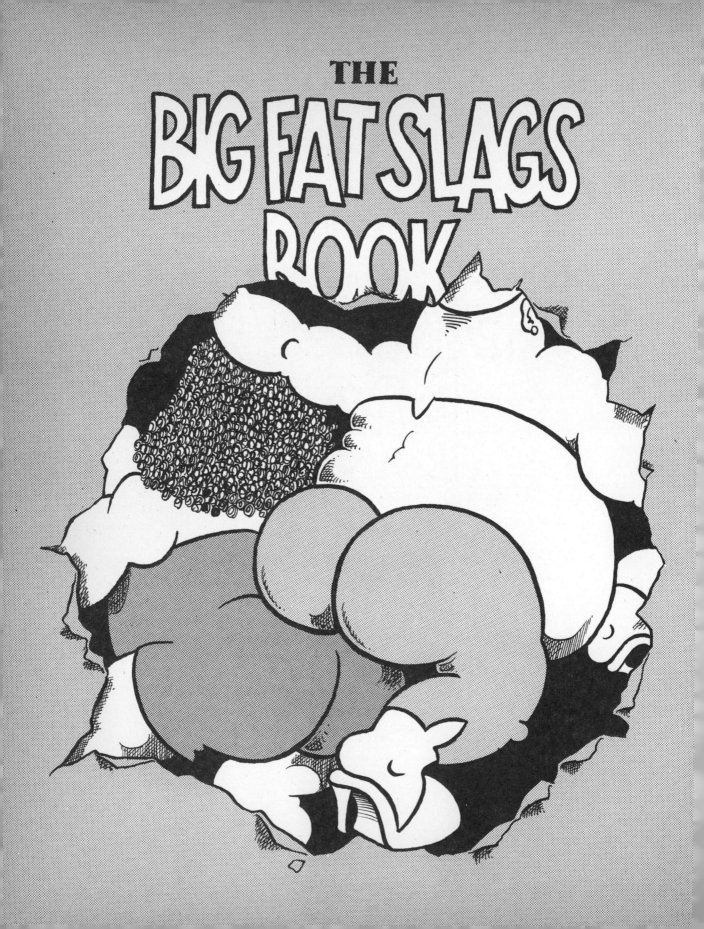

THE BIG FAT SLAGS BOOK

CONTENTS

5

8

9

11

12

16

17

18

19

20

Baz Askwith

NAME: Barrington Geoff Hurst Askwith.
BORN: July 1966, Fulchester Maternity Hospital car park.
HEIGHT: 5' 3⅜".
OCCUPATION: Unemployed, but painter and decorator on the side.
HOBBIES: Smoking, pubs, fishing, real tennis.
FAVE GIRL: Sam Fox, Nicole off the Renault adverts, Bananarama.
FAVE VEHICLE: Ford Capri with rear spoilers and disco lights.
PRESENT VEHICLE: 1977 Cossack Motorcycle and sidecar combination.
FAVE FOOD: Pot Noodle, Kebabs, Vesta boil-in-the-bag curry.
FAVE DRINK: Fulchester Brown Ale.
FAVE TELLY PROGRAMME: Miss World, Baywatch.
FAVE FILMS: Confessions of a Plumber's Mate, Carry on Camping.
FAVE MAGS: Exchange and Mart, Big Fish, Combat and Survival, Razzle.
HOME: Self-contained, upper floor bachelor pad.
AMBITION: To move out of my bedroom in my mam and dad's house, and get me own place. Probably a houseboat like Don Johnston in Miami Vice.
LIKES: The countryside, parties, birds with big tits.
HATES: Sexism, birds with small tits.
FIRST SEXUAL EXPERIENCE: I was fourteen, and was in the garden shed with a topless model.
MOST EMBARRASSING MOMENT: Being caught by my mam having a wank on page 3 of the Sun in the shed when I was fourteen.

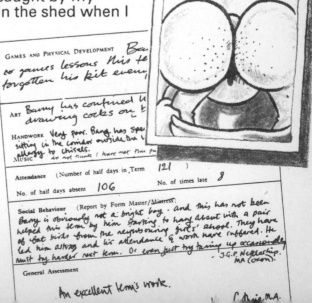

| B.G.H. Askwith | | Term | | Assessment |
Subject	Effort	Marks	Position	
English				Baz not done very well this turn. More work is required next turm.
Reading	E	3%	34	
Spelling	E	4½%	34	
Writing	E	2%	33=	
Comprehension	E	1%	34	He seems keener on reading wank mags than "Tess of the Derbervilles" and Shakespear.
Composition	E	6%	34	
Grammar, etc.	E	3%	34	
Literature	E	½%	34	
History	E	11%	34	Very poor. EH. Extremely poor. Very poor indeed. A poor term's work. Baz is shit.
Geography	E	0%	34	
Religious Knowledge	E	2⅔%	34	
French	E	1%	34	
Latin	E	2%	34	
Arithmetic	E	2%	34	Barrington has attended only one lesson this term and was sent out of...
Mental	E	1%	34	
Mechanical	E	4%	34	
Problems	E	4%	34	

Games and Physical Development Ba... co games lessons this te... forgotten his kit every...

Art Barry has continued t... drawing cocks on t...

Handwork Very poor. Barry has spe... sitting in the corridor outside the... allergy to chisels.

Music do not think I have met this pu...

Attendance (Number of half days in Term 121)

No. of half days absent 106   No. of times late 8

Social Behaviour (Report by Form Master/Mistress)
Barry is obviously not a bright boy, and this has not been helped this term by him starting to hang about with a pair of bad birds from the neighbouring girls' school. They have led him astray and his attendance & work have suffered. He must try harder next term. Or even just try turning up occasionally.
— J.G.P. Nethleship, MA (oxon).

General Assessment
An excellent term's work.
C...rie M.A.

23

24

25

26

27

29

31

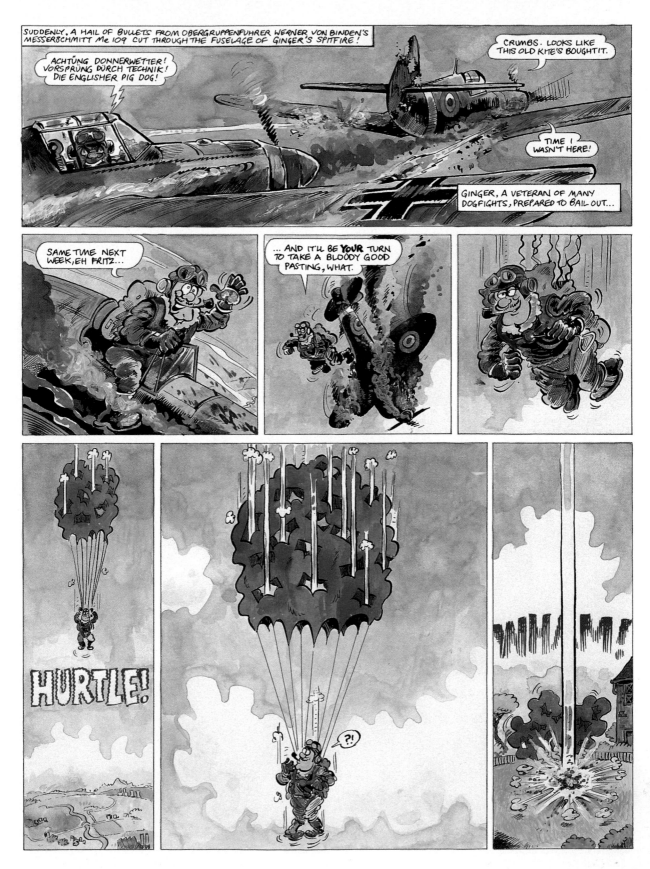

35

36

38

40

42

43

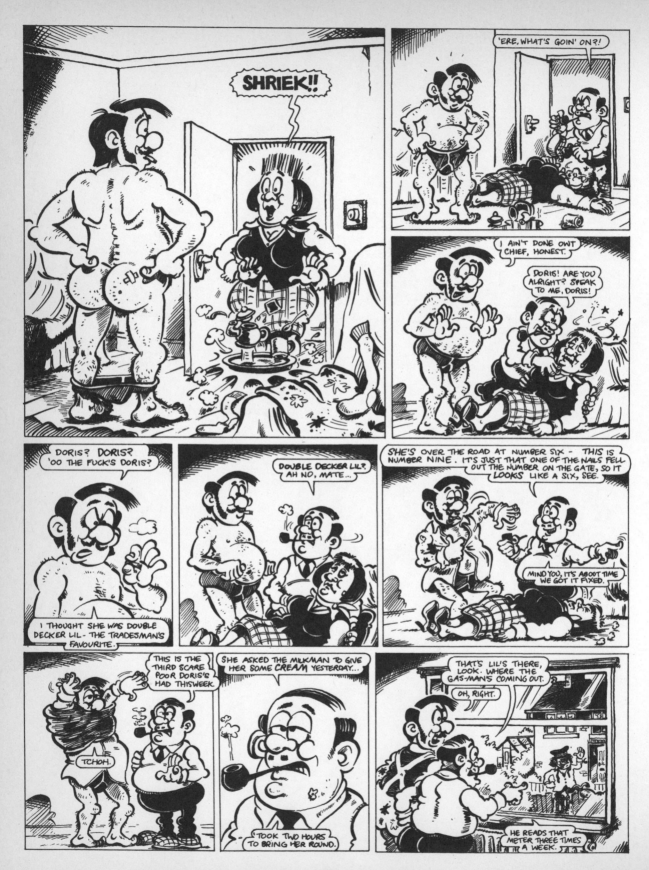

44

45

46

47

48

49

52

54

56

57

58

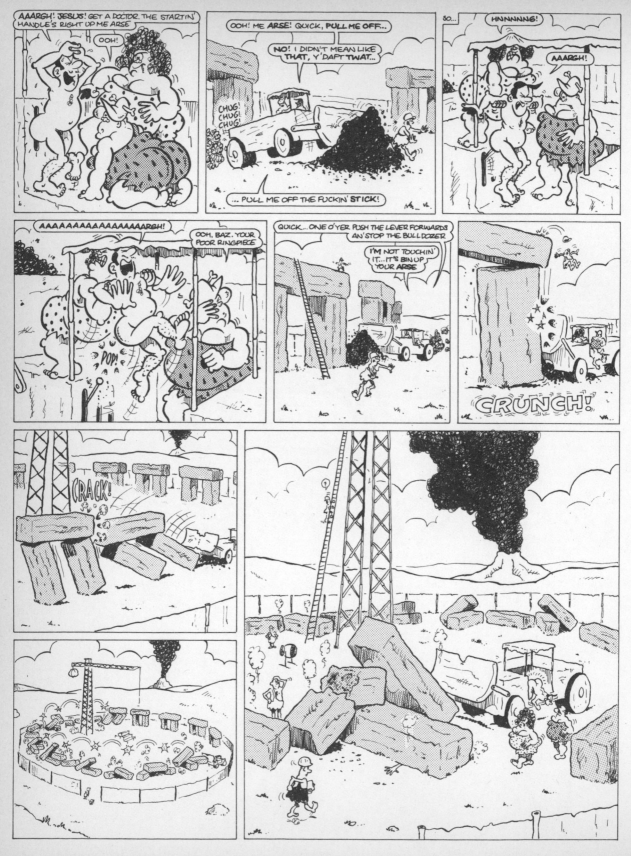

60

61

Visit the toilet.

Miss a turn.

You pay to go in a nightclub only to find that it is a rave, there is no alcohol on the premises and all the blokes are sweaty, dazed-looking fourteen year olds. **Miss a turn.**

You attempt sex in the pub car park with a casual acquaintance who suffers from premature ejaculation. **Miss a turn** whilst you clean the spunk off your dress.

There is no queue at the chip shop and a fresh batch has just come out of the lard. **Advance 3 squares.**

You have Baz up a back and attempt to have sex with him. Throw again to see if he has brewers droop. Odd Number = Droop. **Move back 2 squares.** Even Number = Panhandle **Move forward 2 squares.**

There's a Sambuca promotion on in a pub and you have two pints for the price of one. You feel like you're in a washing machine. **Move forward 3 squares.**

San & Tray's Friday Night Pub Crawl Ga

Happy Hour! Three shots for a quid. **Have another turn.**

You are caught short and have to have a piss in a shop doorway and you splash your knickers. **Move back 2 squares.**

You come across some men on a stag night. The groom has drunk 28 pints and is slipping in and out of a coma, but you manage to pull him off. **Move forward 2 squares.**

You lose Baz in a crowded pub and have to buy your own drink. **Move back 4 squares.**

Visit the toilet.

Miss a turn.

You throw up violently in th back of a taxi **Move forwar 2 squares.**

You corner Baz in a bus stop and attempt to have sex with him. Throw again to see if he has brewers droop. Odd Number = Droop. **Move back 2 squares.** Even Number = Panhandle. **Move forward 2 squares.**

Start

You have no money left for a taxi home, so you offer to pay in kind. **Miss a turn** whilst the cabby feels your tits.

Finish

You go for a curry and Baz shits himself. He throws away his soiled trousers with his wallet in the pocket. YOU have to pay for the meal. **Go back to the start.**

Visit the toilet.

Miss a turn.

You are arrested for being drunk and disorderly. **Miss 2 turns** while several policemen gang bang you in the back of a transit van before releasing you with a caution.

The hunk you have spent ten minutes chatting up turns out to be an arse bandit. **Move back 2 squares.**

You wake up in an alleyway with your knickers in your handbag. You have a thumping headache, you do not know where you are or who you are. **Move forward 4 squares.**

You trap Baz in a 'phone box and attempt to have sex with him. Throw again to see if he has brewers droop.
Odd Number = Droop.
Move back 2 squares.
Even Number = Panhandle.
Move forward 2 squares.

Everybody loves a Friday night piss up. Well now every night can be Friday night with this spectacular Fat Slags Friday night pub crawl game. Simply get two small objects to use as counters, e.g. a button and a sugar cube, roll a dice and away you go. You may like to drink heavily whilst playing the game. The winner is the person who wins.

You avoid paying your bus fare by shagging the conductor, but in doing so, leave an expensive pair of knickers stuffed down the seat. **Stay where you are.**

The doorman at the nightclub lets you in for free after you've pulled him off in the cloakroom. **Move forward 2 squares.**

You order half a lager and lime and the barman accidently gives you the alcohol-free variety. **Move back 2 squares.**

You stagger drunken into the path of a car which screeches to a halt. You bang on the bonnet repeatedly whilst shouting incoherent abuse at the driver before laughing raucously and tottering off. **Move forward 4 squares.**

You come across some women on a hen night and in a drunken stupor, you end up wearing the large cardboard hat with condoms on it. **Move back 2 squares.**

Visit the toilet.

Miss a turn.

You discover that a randy barman has been trying to get you pissed by spiking your drinks and you are legless after three halves of lager. **Have another turn.**

THE RUING STING

FISH N CHIPS

67

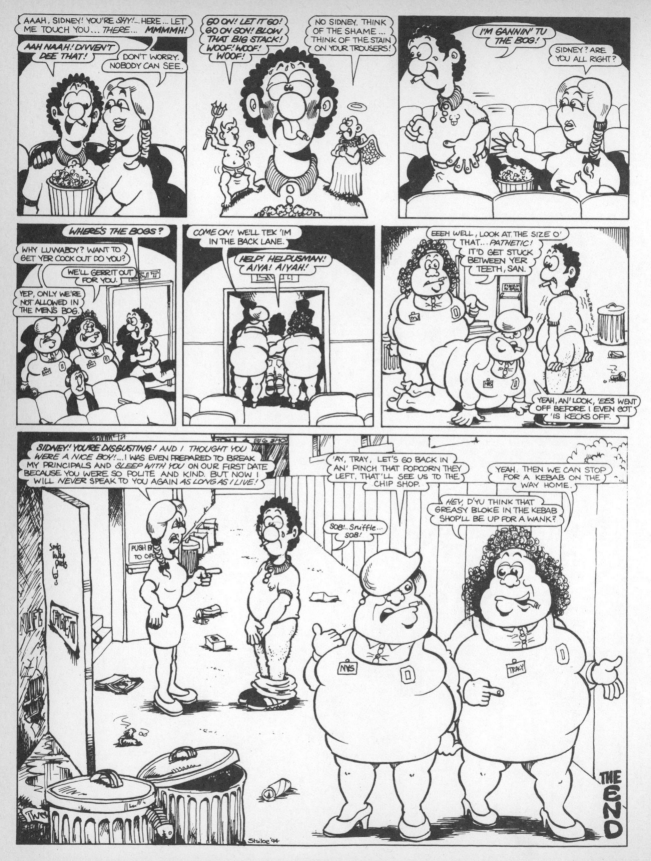

68

72